THAT'S OUR LIBRARIAN!

The author and photographer wish to thank the children and faculty at P.S. 30, Bronx, New York, for their wonderful help and inspiration in the preparation of this book. Special thanks to Stephen Brown for all his wonderful help and support in the preparation of the manuscript.

Library of Congress Cataloging-in-Publication Data

Morris, Ann, 1930–
That's our librarian!/Ann Morris ; photographs and illustrations by Peter Linenthal.
p. cm.—(That's our school)
Summary: Introduces Maria Rodriguez, an elementary school librarian, describing what she does during the school day and how she interacts with other staff and students.
ISBN 0-7613-2400-3 (lib. bdg.)
1. School librarians—Juvenile literature. [1. School librarians. 2. Librarians. 3. Occupations.] I. Linenthal, Peter, ill. II. Title.
Z682.4.S34 M67 2003
027.8—dc21   2002152488

The Millbrook Press, Inc.
2 Old New Milford Road
Brookfield, Connecticut 06804
www.millbrookpress.com

THAT'S OUR SCHOOL

THAT'S OUR LIBRARIAN!

Ann Morris

Photographs and Illustrations
by Peter Linenthal

The Millbrook Press / Brookfield, Connecticut

Our school is in the Bronx,
a part of New York City.
We think the Bronx is a
great place to live.
We have the best librarian,
Maria Rodriguez.
We think she's cool
and we love her!
"Hello, boys and girls,"
she says as we come
to her door.

Our librarian loves to read.
She helps us learn to
love reading, too.
Often she reads us stories.

Our librarian always makes us
feel at home in her library.
She helps us find out information
about things we are learning in school.
She helps us find the right
books to read on our own.
We check out the books
we want to borrow at her desk.
"Hope you like the book," she says.

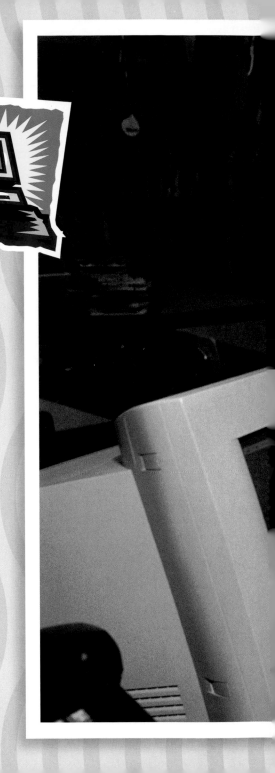

Our librarian does many
different things in her job.
She chooses books for our library
and orders them with our principal.

She keeps track of all the books in the library. To do this, she must take care of many papers and files.

Our librarian also meets with our
teachers to plan special events.

She helps us learn to use computers. Sometimes she even gives computer lessons to our PTA president.

Our librarian speaks Spanish and English. Many children in our school speak Spanish and English, too. Our librarian makes sure our library has plenty of books in both languages.

¿HABLA ESPAÑOL?

Our librarian sometimes invites children's book authors to our school. They visit our classrooms and talk with us about the books they write.

It's fun talking to authors about their books!

Our librarian
often stops by
the lunchroom
to talk with us.

For our Easter party
she brought a cake
shaped as a bunny.

At our Halloween party, our librarian came as Dorothy in the Wizard of Oz.

At our school we celebrate Three Kings' Day at Christmastime. At this celebration everybody sings and claps their hands in time to the music. Mrs. Rodriguez enjoyed the time that one of our neighbors brought his own instrument, called a *guiro*, and sang along with us.

A very young child came, too,
and beat the conga drum.

The Rodriguez family at home—Jose, Mrs. Rodriguez, and Nikita behind Luis, Xavier and Julius.

Mrs. Rodriguez has five children—
Luis, Xavier, and Julius, who are triplets,
and Jose and Nikita, who are both older.

The family lives in Washington Heights, another part of New York City not far from the Bronx. This is their apartment building.

The family has a lot of fun together . . . reading, bowling,

and eating pizza.

Mrs. Rodriguez's twin sister, Rosa Veras, is also a teacher in our school. The sisters grew up in the Dominican Republic, an island country near Florida. When they were younger, they shared many things—even their birthday cake! The sisters still do many things together.

Mrs. Rodriguez and her sister when they were girls

Mrs. Rodriguez and her twin sister in the Dominican Republic

When Mrs. Rodriguez and her family go on vacation, her sister sometimes comes along. Mrs. Rodriguez told us she has wonderful times on her vacations.

But we're always glad when
Mrs. Rodriguez comes
back to us.
Often she brings books
and stories to share!
There she is.
THAT'S OUR LIBRARIAN!

THINGS TO DO

Would you like to
know more about
your school librarian
or what it is like
to be a librarian?

Would you like to do
something nice for
your school librarian?

Try one of these
activities.

Learn About Your Librarian

- Interview your school librarian.
  Find out all the things a librarian does.

- Invite your librarian into your classroom.
  Ask what kinds of books she or he likes
  to read.

Make a Book, Bookmark, or Book Plate

- Make a book for your school librarian. Invite your librarian to your classroom and give it to her or him.

- Make a book for your classroom library. Read it to your classmates.

- Make a bookmark with your own design.

- Make a book plate with your name on it. You can make copies on a copy machine. Paste them into all of your own books.

Make a Classroom Library

- Bring your favorite books from home and set up a library in a corner of your classroom.

- Make library cards with pictures of each student on the cards.

- Make a library card holder to protect your card.

- Make an I LOVE TO READ poster for your classroom.

- Take turns being the "Librarian for a Day" in your classroom library.

About the Author

Ann Morris loves children, and she loves writing books
for children. She has written more than eighty books for
children, including a series of books for The Millbrook
Press about grandmothers and their grandchildren called
What Was It Like, Grandma? For many years Ann Morris
taught school. Eventually, she left teaching to become
an editor with a children's book publishing company.
While she still sometimes teaches workshops and
seminars for teachers, Ann Morris now spends most
of her time writing. She lives in New York City.

About the Photographer-Illustrator

Peter Linenthal is a talented photographer and illustrator.
He studied fine arts at the San Francisco Art Institute.
He is a native of California and teaches at the San Francisco
Center for the Book. Peter Linenthal also loves children
and working on books for children. He did the photographs
and illustrations for Ann Morris's books about grandmothers.